Paradise for God

St. Alphonsus de Liguori and the Spirituality of Heart

Dennis J. Billy, C.Ss.R.

En Route Books and Media, LLC
Saint Louis, MO

En Route Books and Media, LLC
5705 Rhodes Avenue
St. Louis, MO 63109

Contact us at
contactus@enroutebooksandmedia.com

Cover Credit: Sebastian Mahfood

Copyright 2026 Dennis J. Billy, C.Ss.R.

ISBN-13: 979-8-88870-435-6
Library of Congress Control Number: 2025947062

All rights reserved. No part of this book may be reproduced, stored in a retrieval system, or transmitted in any form, or by any means, electronic, mechanical, photocopying, or otherwise, without the prior written permission of the author.

For the Redemptorist Partners in Mission

The paradise of God…
is the heart of man.

St. Alphonsus de Liguori (1696-1787)

Table of Contents

Introduction 1

Chapter One: Alphonsus's Spirituality of Heart 5

Chapter Two: Exploring the Human Heart 23

Chapter Three: Prayer, The Great Means of

    Salvation 41

Chapter Four: Friendship with God 61

Chapter Five: Paradise for God 79

Conclusion 95

Introduction

Alphonsian spirituality has been likened to a double-edged sword, with one blade signifying a "spirituality of practice;" the other, a "spirituality of heart;" both of which come together in a single point representing a "spirituality of mission." This metaphor stems from an incident in Alphonsus's life when, after a time of searching about the purpose of his life, he entered the Church of Our Lady of Ransom in Naples and laid his nobleman's sword at the foot of the altar in honor of Our Lady of Mercy, promising her that he would dedicate the rest of his life as a priest filled with zeal for the salvation of souls. This event resonates with a verse in Hebrews: "Indeed, the word of God is living and active, sharper than any two-edged sword, piercing until it divides the soul from spirit, joints from marrow; it can judge the thoughts and intentions of the heart" (Heb 4:12).[1] In a previous work, *Holy Exercises*, we examined

---

[1] All Scripture quotations come from *Holy Bible: New Revised Standard Version with Apocrypha* (New York: Oxford University Press, 1989).

Alphonsus's "spirituality of practice."[2] This present work, *Paradise for God,* will look at his "spirituality of heart."

The book is comprised of five chapters. Chapter one, "Alphonsus's Spirituality of Heart," examines the Biblical meaning of "heart," its relevance for Alphonsus, and how he envisions practice as a way of accessing it and bringing about fundamental conversion (*metanoia*) in a person's life. Chapter two, "Exploring the Human Heart," takes an anthropological approach to the concept of "heart" and looks at how Alphonsus's approach to mental prayer and his *Way of the Cross* touch upon every dimension of our human makeup. Chapter three, "Prayer, the Great Means of Salvation," identifies prayer, both communal and personal, as the primary way to access the heart, looks at why Alphonsus focused on the various ascetical forms of prayers, and considers why mental prayer is morally necessary for salvation. Chapter four, "Friendship with God," considers the

---

[2] See Dennis J. Billy, *Holy Exercises: Alphonsus de Liguori and the Spirituality of Practice* (St. Louis, MO: En Route Books and Media, 2024).

final end of the spiritual life. For Alphonsus, the whole purpose of accessing our heart is to turn it away from a life of sin and self-centeredness and open it to an intimate relationship with Jesus and his Spirit. Chapter five, "Paradise for God," looks at God's deepest desire and explores how by sharing in our humanity he allows us to share in his divinity. The Conclusion offers a precise summary of Alphonsus's "spirituality of heart," and points to its ramification for his "spirituality of mission."

Pope Francis's insights in his encyclical *Delexit nos, on the Human and Divine Love of the Heart of Jesus* (October 24, 2024)[3] reinforce the relevance of Alphonsus's "spirituality of heart" for the Church's continuing efforts at evangelization. May this book inspire all members of the Redemptorist family to follow in the footsteps of the Redeemer in their own day, as Alphonsus so ardently tried to do so in his.

---

[3] Pope Francis, *Delexit nos: On the Human and Divine Love of the Heart of Jesus* (Encyclical letter, October 24, 2024). https://www.vatican.va/content/francesco/en/encyclicals/documents/20241024-enciclica-dilexit-nos.html.

Chapter One

Alphonsus's Spirituality of Heart

Alphonsus's "spirituality of heart" presupposes a "spirituality of practice." The human heart, in other words, is penetrated, touched, and ultimately transformed by the grace-filled repetition of holy exercises that exist for the expressed purpose of bringing about a fundamental conversion (*metanoia*) in a person's life. The sole purpose of these devout practices is to turn stony hearts into natural hearts. Jesus came to fulfill the words of the prophet:

> "A new heart I will give you, and a new spirit I will put within you; and I will remove from your body the heart of stone and give you a heart of flesh. I will put my spirit within you and make you follow my statutes and be careful to observe my ordinances" (Ez 36: 26-27).

In this chapter, we will explore Alphonsus's understanding of the meaning of "heart" and treat in more detail the contours of what precisely a "spirituality of heart" entails.

The Meaning of "Heart"

Before treating Alphonsus's understanding of the "spirituality of heart," it will be helpful to look at how the Christian philosophical and spiritual tradition considers it in general. In his book *Heart of the World*, Hans Urs von Balthasar (1905-88) gives us a succinct summary of its meaning: "Both Biblically and philosophically (in the total human context, that is) the heart is conceived as the real center of spiritual and corporeal man, and, by analogy, it is also seen as the very center of God as he opens himself up to man."[1] As far as the Scriptures are concerned, he writes:

> In the Old Testament, the heart is still largely understood as the seat of spiritual energy and of thought, while the bosom or "bowels" (as in "bowels of mercy": *rachamim, splanchna*) are rather taken to be the seat of affections. In the New Testament, however, both aspects coincide with the concept of "heart." Having one's "whole

---

[1] Hans Urs von Balthasaar, *Heart of the World*, trans. Erasmo S. Leiva (San Francisco: Ignatius Press, 1979), 14.

heart" turned to God means the opening of the man towards him (Acts 8:37; Mt 22:37). Thus, the heart that was hardened (Mk 10:5), following numerous parallels in the Old Testament must be renewed: from a stony heart it must become a heart of flesh (Ez 11:19, etc.; cf. 2 Cor 3:3).[2]

While Greek philosophy saw the heart as "the center of psychic and spiritual life,"[3] the New Testament, according to Balthasaar, adds a decidedly incarnational aspect to it:

"The soul is wholly incarnate in the heart, and, in the heart, the body wholly becomes the medium for the expression of the soul. At the same time, the New Testament adds an element of personhood: it is first in Christianity that the entire man—body and soul—becomes a unique person through God's call and, with his heart, orients towards God this uniqueness that is his."[4]

---

[2] Ibid.

[3] Ibid.

[4] Ibid., 14-15.

More recently, Pope Francis (1936-2025), in *Dilexit nos*, his encyclical on the human and divine heart of Jesus Christ, offers a succinct summary of the meaning of heart, one that affirms previous magisterial teaching and its relevance for today's world:

> The word "heart" proves its value for philosophy and theology in their efforts to reach an integral synthesis. Nor can its meaning be exhausted by biology, psychology, anthropology or any other science. It is one of those primordial words that "describe realities belonging to man precisely in so far as he is one whole (as a corporeo-spiritual person)." It follows that biologists are not being more "realistic" when they discuss the heart, since they see only one aspect of it; the whole is not less real, but even more real. Nor can abstract language ever acquire the same concrete and integrative meaning. The word "heart" evokes the inmost core of our person, and thus it enables us to understand ourselves in our integrity and not merely under one isolated aspect.[5]

---

[5] Pope Francis, *Delixit nos*, no. 15.

These remarks from von Balthasar and Pope Francis underscore both the importance and relevance of the concept of "heart" for the Christian tradition. It is an understanding with which Alphonsus was familiar and took for granted. What is more, the notion of *metanoia* (fundamental conversion of heart) lies at the very center of his missionary strategy.

The Meaning of "Heart" in Alphonsus

St. Alphonsus was someone steeped in the tradition of the Church and was doubtless aware of the meaning of "heart," having made many references to it from Scripture, Tradition, Church fathers, saints, doctors, and teachings of the various Church councils.

Alphonsus, however, does not merely accept the traditional Catholic understanding of "heart" as the inmost core of a person that allows the soul to incarnate itself in and through the body, but he also deepens our understanding of it by tying it to the underlying Gospel narrative that Jesus entered our world in the mystery of the Incarnation (Crib), gave himself completely to us in the mystery of his Passion and

Death (Cross), became a source of nourishment for us in the mystery of the Eucharist (Sacrament), and became a source of hope for us in the mysteries of his Resurrection and Ascension (Mary). Mary embodies the latter mysteries because in being assumed body and soul into heaven at the end of her earthly sojourn, she alone of all human beings has, at this very moment, experienced the fullness of redemption. She has thus become a source of hope for us that we, too, might one day be fully redeemed in both body and soul. In this respect, she remains, as the words of the *Salve Regina* remind us, "our life, our sweetness, and our hope."

This underlying Gospel narrative lies at the center of Alphonsus's spirituality of heart and represents a movement of the Father's heart as manifested in the heart of his Son. Jesus' redeeming purpose is to enter our hearts by the power of his Spirit, befriend us, heal our nature, wounded as it is by the effects of original sin, and elevate us by allowing us to share in his glorified humanity. The Father's heart, in other words, was one with Jesus' heart, and through the mysteries of his Incarnation, passion and death, the sacrament of the Eucharist, and the mysteries of his

Resurrection and Ascension, empowers us to become God's adopted sons and daughters. This underlying Gospel narrative, moreover, is already at work in our lives and sends us forth as Jesus' disciples to enter the worlds of those around us and give ourselves completely to them in order to become nourishment for them and a source of hope. When seen in this light, we are called to follow in the footsteps of Mary, Jesus' first and closest disciple, whose one and only desire is to lead others to her Son. In sharing in his heart-filled Gospel narrative, we are spreading Jesus' Gospel message that the kingdom of God is both in our midst and in our hearts.

The Hearts of Jesus and Mary

For Alphonsus, Jesus' heart is the model *par excellence* of what we should desire our hearts to be like. In his *Novena to the Sacred Heart of Jesus* (1758), he writes:

> His heart is all pure, all holy, and all full of love toward God and toward us. This is because he desires only the glory of the Father and our own good. His is the heart in which God finds all delight. Every

perfection, every virtue, reign in the heart of Jesus. In it we find a most ardent love or God the Father, together with the greatest spirit of humility and respect possible. In it we discover a saving understanding of our sins which he has taken upon himself, united to the fullest confidence of a most loving Son. In it at the same time, we find a total abhorrence of our sins united to a deep recognition of our weaknesses. In it, too, we see a great sadness united to perfect conformity to the will of God.[6]

Jesus' heart represents all that God wishes us to become. He sent his Son into the world not only to free us from Satan's hold, but also to set our hearts on fire with love for him and to give us a share in his glorified humanity. Although we were created in God's image and likeness (Gn 2:26), that image became tarnished by Adam's fall, the consequences of which have been passed down from generation to generation. Jesus entered our world to heal us of this deep wound in our human nature, completely transform

---

[6] Alphonsus de Liguori, *Novena to the Sacred Heart of Jesus* in From the Heart of Saint Alphonsus: Favorite Devotions from the Doctor of Prayer, ed. Norman J. Muckerman (Liguori, MO: Liguori Publications, 2002), 27.

Chapter One: Alphonsus's Spirituality of Heart

us (recreate us, if you will), and enable us to follow in his footsteps. When his heart was pierced on the cross, the blood and water flowing from his side revealed to us the deepest meaning of love: "This is my commandment, that you love one another as I have loved you. No one has greater love than this, to lay down one's life for one's friends" (Jn 15:12-13). Jesus desires to be our closest and most intimate friend: "You are my friends if you do what I command you" (Jn 15:14). He sought nothing more than to do the will of his heavenly Father: "The Father and I are one" (Jn 10: 30). He wishes the same for us and seeks to do so by joining his heart to ours through the bond of friendship. Jesus, in other words, wishes to dwell deep within our hearts so that we can dwell in his.

Of all the human persons who ever lived, no one was closer to Jesus than his mother. Mary was his first and closest disciple. She was with him from the moment he was conceived in her womb to his death on the cross on Golgotha. She was with him throughout his hidden life in Nazareth and throughout his public ministry. Her heart was pierced with the sword of sorrow as his was pierced by a lance. She was with him when he was laid in the freshly hewn tomb and now sits at his right hand as Queen of heaven and earth. Her heart was on fire with the love of her Son. Of all human beings who ever lived, she alone has experienced the fullness of redemption. According to Alphonsus, her answer to the angel's message is the embodiment of what it means to be a humble servant of the Lord:

> Let us see the great humility of Mary in this answer. She was fully enlightened as to the greatness of the dignity of the mother of God. She had already been assured by the angel that she was this mother chosen by the Lord. Nevertheless, in spite of this, she does not rise in her own estimation, she does not stop to rejoice in her exaltation. Aware of her own nothingness on the one hand, and of the infinite majesty of God who chose her to be his mother on the other, she acknowledges herself to be unworthy of such a great honor; yet she has not the slightest wish to oppose his will. So, when she is asked for her consent, what does she do? What does she say? Wholly annihilated within herself, and yet at the same time inflamed by the desire to unite herself still more closely to God, abandoning herself completely to the divine will, she says, *Behold the handmaid of the Lord.* Behold the *slave* of the Lord,

obliged to do whatever the Lord commands. It is as if she intended to say: Since God chooses for his mother one who has nothing of her own, and since all that I have I have received from him, who could ever think that he has chosen me because of my merits. *Behold the handmaid of the Lord.* How could a slave ever possibly merit to become the mother of her Lord? *Behold the handmaid of the Lord.* May the goodness of the Lord alone be praised, and not his slave, since it is due to his goodness alone that he has cast his eyes on a creature as lowly as I am with a view to making her so great.[7]

If Mary looks constantly to her Son, her Son wants us to look at him though his mother's gentle, loving gaze. She desires one thing and one thing only: to lead others to him. Mary, moreover, is not only Mother of God but also Mother of the Church, the Mother of each and every one of us. At the wedding feast of Cana, she has her Son's ear (Jn 23:1-11). He listens to her requests and takes them seriously. For this reason, we can turn to her in time of need and

---

[7] Alphonsus de Liguori, *The Glories of Mary: A New Translation* from the Italian (Liguori, MO: Liguori Publications, 2000), 223-24.

know that she will intercede with her Son on our behalf. She is one with her Son and therefore one with our heavenly Father. She is full of the Holy Spirit and full of grace. If Jesus is the New Adam, then she is the New Eve. If the saints were known as the "friends of God"[8] in the early Church, we can rest assured that she was not only Jesus' mother, but also his closest and most intimate friend.

Healing Our Wounded Hearts

If Jesus and his mother, Mary, embody those who are pure of heart, we by way of contrast, belong to the rest of humanity, that great mass of people who, because of Adam's fall from grace, are weak and brokenhearted. With the Apostle Paul, each of us say to ourselves deep down inside, "I do not understand my own actions. For I do not do what I want, but I do the very thing I hate" (Rom 7:15). The only remedy for this is to humbly approach the Lord and seek his forgiveness. Alphonsus de Liguori puts it this way:

---

[8] See Peter Brown, *The Making of Late Antiquity* (Cambridge, MA: Harvard University Press, 1978), 54-80.

> But you know not how to despise a heart that repents and humbles itself: "A contrite and humble heart, O God, You will not despise" (Ps 50:19). Ah, now, indeed, neither in this life nor in the other do I desire any but You alone: "What have I in heaven? and besides You what do I desire upon earth! You are the God of my heart, and the God that is my portion forever" (Ps 72:25). You alone are and shall be forever the only Lord of my heart, of my will; You my only good, my heaven, my hope, my love, my all: "The God of my heart, and the God that is my portion forever."[9]

Jesus desires nothing more than to be the Lord of our hearts. He created our world and everything in it for no other reason than to befriend us. Unlike the rest of the created world, he made us *capax Dei*, capable of entering into a relationship with him. When our first parents went astray at the dawn of time, he made things right by entering our world, giving himself

---

[9] Alphonsus de Liguori, *The Way to Converse Always and Familiarly with God*, in *Talking with God: Four Treatises on the Interior Life* from St. Alphonsus Liguori (Mesa, AZ: Scriptoria Books, 2011), 5-6.

completely to us to the point of death, becoming nourishment for us, and a source of hope. And he did all this because he wishes to enter our world and dwell within our hearts so that we might dwell in his. He loves us beyond all telling. In the words of Alphonsus, "The paradise of God, so to speak, is the heart of man."[10]

Only God can heal our wounded hearts; only he can make us whole. By becoming one of us and dying on the cross, he took upon himself all our wounds and then healed and transformed them. He is our "Wounded Healer," as Henri Nouwen (1932-96) would have it, who bears the wounds of his crucifixion in his risen and glorified humanity. In the person of Jesus, God embraced our broken humanity so that we could one day share in his glorified divinity. As Athanasius of Alexandria (d. 373) puts it, God "became man so that man might become divine."[11] That is to say that, because of Jesus' paschal mystery, we can now participate in God's intimate community of Love. We do not become God but are transformed into divinized human beings who share in Jesus'

---

[10] Ibid., 7.
[11] Athanasius of Alexandria, *De incarnatione*, 54.3.

glorified human nature. As a result, we share in the love of the Father for the Son and that of the Son for the Father. We share in this bond because the Holy Spirit, who embodies the love between the Father and the Son, now dwells in our hearts and allows us to dwell in Jesus' heart and the heart of the Father.

Interestingly enough, our first parents, Adam and Eve, ate the forbidden fruit from the tree of the knowledge of good and evil, thinking that, by doing so, they would become like God (Gn 3:5). What they took for themselves out of pride and selfishness, God ends up giving it to us freely out of his deep love for us, whom he created in his image and likeness (Gn 1:26). Another way of saying this is that, through Jesus, God has given us the opportunity to become his friends. Our relationship with him bears the three essential marks of friendship[12]—benevolence, reciprocity, and mutual indwelling—and we can, once again, open our hearts and speak freely to him, as close friends often do. Because of Jesus, the fellowship with God that was broken and lost by our first

---

[12] See Paul J. Wadell, *Friendship and the Moral Life* (Notre Dame, IN: University of Notre Dame Press, 1989), 130-41.

parents was finally restored, once and for all. Because of him, we now can carry his love within our hearts. He dwells in our hearts—and we in his. As with the early saints of old, we, too, can be known as the "friends of God." Our relationship with him is all but ours to lose.

The closer we draw near to Christ, the more will we become like him. Our relationship with him never remains static: it is either waxing or waning, becoming closer or more distant. We are either growing in holiness or not. It is impossible to stand still in the spiritual life. To become a saint involves letting go of our petty wishes and sinful desires and allowing him to reign in our hearts. Jesus is king of all the earth and all the universe. His deepest desire, however, is to reign in our hearts through the power of his Spirit. When his Spirit dwells within our hearts, we become the persons he has always envisioned us to be. We are gradually freed of the desires of the flesh, slowly transformed into highly polished images of our Incarnate God, and eventually transformed into divinized human beings, who share in Jesus' glorified humanity.

Conclusion

The concept of "heart" has deep roots in Western civilization, as well as in the Judeo-Christian tradition. It signifies the deepest dimension of the human person, the center of one's selfhood, capable of opening up to God and entering into relationship with him. It embraces our entire being, both body and soul, and is unique to each one of us. The heart is capable of change. It can turn us toward God or away from him. Because of it, we can draw closer to ourselves and others, or farther away. The choice is ours to make.

St. Alphonsus was aware of the traditional Christian understanding of heart and uses the word throughout his literary corpus. He comes to a deeper understanding of its meaning by tying it to the underlying Gospel narrative that he identifies, and which forms a part of his fundamental missionary orientation: to bring about *metanoia*, a fundamental change in a person's heart. He says that Jesus and Mary, his mother, are examples *par excellence* of what it means to be single-hearted and pure of heart, and he holds them up as models to emulate in our own spiritual lives.

Unlike Jesus and Mary, however, we have been wounded by the consequences of Adam's fall from grace and, as a result, have a difficult time of purifying our hearts and walking in the state of grace. To rectify this situation, the Word of God entered our world by taking on human flesh and preparing in Mary a suitable place for him to be conceived so as to enter our world unblemished by sin. He came to heal our wounds, befriend us, and share his divine life with us. Jesus wishes nothing more than to live in our hearts, and he in ours. St. Alphonsus's "spirituality of heart" focuses on this divine purpose. He mentions, time and again, that we are capable of God (*capax Dei*) and able to share in his divinity. In the next chapter, we will explore the various dimensions of the human heart in more detail.

Chapter Two

Exploring the Human Heart

Alphonsus's spirituality embraces every dimension of the heart: the physical, psychological/intellectual, spiritual, communal, and environmental. To better understand how he addresses each of these aspects, let us look at each of them one-by-one and then see how he integrates them into a single whole through two of his best-known holy exercises: the practice of mental prayer and his *Way of the Cross*.[1] In doing so, we shall see that Alphonsus was interested in the conversion of the whole person and that his writings on prayer manifest a deep concern for both the individual and his or her relationship to the larger community.

---

[1] See St. Alphonsus Liguori, *Mental Prayer* in Talking with God, 63-108; St. Alphonsus de Liguori, *Way of the Cross* in The Complete Ascetical Works of St. Alphonsus de Liguori, ed. Eugene Grimm, vol. 5 (Brooklyn, Redemptorist Fathers, 1927), 479-91.

An Anthropology of Heart

Although the human heart is more than just a biological organ, every other meaning ascribed to it flows from the all-important role it plays in our human anatomy: pumping oxygen-rich blood throughout the body while at the same time removing the waste our bodies produce. The heart is one of our most important physical organs; we cannot live without it. It is a symbol of life and therefore of all the good things in it. By way of analogy, people without a heart are dead to the other dimensions of their human makeup.

The Physical. Without the heart pumping blood throughout the rest of our body, we would not have the essential elements that keep us alive and enable us to live on this earth and prosper as human beings. Without it, we would not be able to inhale and exhale, love and procreate, work and play, cook and eat, sleep and dream, or do any of the other daily activities we normally take for granted. The heart is a *sine qua non* of human survival, something so fundamental to life that we should be grateful for having one and willing to take the necessary steps to care for it.

A person with a healthy heart can hope to live a long life filled with the things that make life worth living. Without one, a person cannot even begin to dream about the future, for he or she can have no future.

The Psychological/Intellectual. Of all the organs to which the heart pumps blood, the brain numbers among (if not *the*) most important. The fact that doctors define death by either the heart stopping to beat or the end of brain activity shows its importance for human life. Although the soul permeates the whole body, it is closely associated with the brain since that organ coordinates our abilities to think, will, imagine, remember, feel, and sense. Someone with poor brain functioning, such as a person with Alzheimer's, will be unable to think clearly and decide upon a proper course of action, let alone remember. Because the heart supplies blood to the brain, it has become closely associated with it, especially with its capacity to love and have deep feelings for someone. When seen in this light, a person of heart is someone who has integrated the rational and appetitive dimensions of the soul and allowed them to act as one.

The Spiritual. When the heart beats, it both expands and contracts. At each end of this movement, it must come to a brief rest before it begins moving in the opposite direction. This moment of rest allows the heart to orient itself in such a way that it can take into some of its chambers blood rich in oxygen and let our unwanted waste in others. This restful stillness corresponds to the spiritual dimension of out human makeup. We need stillness, what Eastern Christianity refers to *hesychia*, a Greek word meaning "stillness," "silence," "quiet" and "rest." This spiritual meaning of "heart" represents the deepest dimension of the human person, one that allows us to commune with God and rest in his presence. It places stillness at the very center of the heart's proper functioning. Without it, the heart would not be able to expand and contract in its pumping activity.

The Communal. The heart is a complex organ with four valves and chambers coordinated in such a way as to make its pumping activity possible. The heart's proper functioning depends on each of these elements to fulfill its proper role. There is thus a communal aspect to the heart, one that requires each of the organ's members to properly perform its designated task. When seen in this light, a wider understanding of heart has an important relational dimension to it, one that deals with proper relations with both God and others. If blood is a symbol of life, then the heart gives life to us and enables us to enter into relationships with others. For this reason, the heart has become a symbol of love. Because of it, we are not only kept alive but also able to establish friendships, raise families, participate in community, and live in society.

The Environmental. The human heart is made of earth: "[Y]ou are dust, and to dust you shall return," we are told in the Book of Genesis (Gn 3:19). As such, we are a part of creation and therefore stand in relationship to the environment. As the pinnacle of God's creation, we are called to be stewards of the earth, not exploiters of it. Our dominion over the earth's resources is meant to be one of preservation. Adam and Eve were placed in the Garden of Eden to care for it rather than to take advantage of it. Because of our first parents, our hearts have been turned around (twisted, you might say), and we have used the earth for our sole benefit and not for the good of the world in which we live. Rather than being caretakers of the world's garden, we have become its abusers. We have taken advantage of what has been placed under our care, and the reason why is because we have turned our hearts inward upon ourselves rather than outward toward others and the world around us.

The human heart has a literal, biological meaning but, by way of extension, many other equally valid applications to the various dimensions of our human makeup. This anthropological understanding of heart will help us to understand more deeply St. Alphonsus's "spirituality of heart." We shall do so by showing how both his manner of making mental prayer and his famous *Stations of the* Cross touch upon each of these dimensions of human existence.

Alphonsus on Mental Prayer

According to Alphonsus, mental prayer is morally necessary for salvation. That is to say it, would be very difficult for us to find our way to God if we do not open or hearts to him. Mental prayer, he says, enlightens the mind. He makes note of what many of the saints have to say about it. St. Augustine of Hippo (354-430), for example, says that those who keep their eyes shut cannot find their way to their home-

Chapter Two: Exploring the Human Heart

land. For St. Bonaventure (1221-74), mental prayer is like a mirror that reveals to us the various stains on our soul. St. Teresa of Avila (1515-82) says it opens our eyes and reveals our imperfections to us. St. Bernard of Clairvaux (1090-1153) says meditation prepares the soul for a time of pruning.[2]

Mental prayer, according to Alphonsus, not only enlightens the mind, but also disposes the heart to practice the virtues. Without it, we would not be able to resist temptation and walk the way of sanctity. He likens it to a fire that enflames the soul with God's love and empowers it to overcome the powers of darkness and the deceit of the evil one. What is more, it helps us to pray as we should by encouraging us to bring to God our every need, from the smallest and seemingly most insignificant to the deepest need of our hearts, our need for God. Mental prayer, for Alphonsus, is the bread and butter of the spiritual life. It is not meant for a select few (such as the clergy and religious) but something we all must do if we wish to find our way to God. It is impossible to become a saint, he says, without mental prayer, the ends of which are to unite ourselves to God and to obtain

---

[2] Ibid., 65-67.

from him the graces necessary for salvation. What is more, we should not seek spiritual consolations but rather try to persevere in holiness in the hope of one day seeing God face to face. The principal objects of mental prayer are the four last things: death, judgment, heaven, and hell. Christ's passion and death and his paschal mystery are also appropriate subjects for meditation.[3]

Alphonsus's approach to mental prayer, moreover, embraces every dimension of our human makeup. He says we can do it anywhere, whether at home or at work, whether sitting or kneeling, walking or working. Some people, he states, prefer doing it the quiet of their rooms; others, before the Blessed Sacrament in a church or chapel. "Solitude of heart," he says, is most important requirement for mental prayer. He refers to St. Gregory the Great's (d. 604) statement that it would profit us little if we were in a solitary place, but our hearts were not free from worldly thoughts and affections. Deserts and caves, in other words, are not necessary for mental prayer. St. Catherine of Siena (1347-80), according to Alphonsus, was able to find God in the midst of her

---

[3] Ibid., 67-86.

daily household activities. According to St. Bernard of Clairvaux, silence and the absence of noise enables the soul to ponder the things of heaven. As far as the time for mental prayer is concerned, Alphonsus says the most important thing is to consider when to do it and for how long. While he emphasizes the fact that we can turn to God at any time, he says that, for St. Bonaventure, morning and evening are the times most conducive to turning to God in prayer. St. Gregory of Nyssa (c. 335-c. 94), by way of contrast, prefers the morning hours to be the best time for it. St. Jerome, moreover, says we should also meditate in the evening. The amount of time spent in mental prayer varies from person to person. Many of the saints would spend any free time they had doing so. Others would do so for an hour in the morning and a half hour in the evening. Still others would do so for shorter intervals of time. Alphonsus reminds us that mental prayer is tedious for those with worldly attachments but easy for those occupied with heavenly things. He reminds us that we can turn to God at any time and for however long we wish. He is our constant companion who is willing to converse with us at any time and place and about any subject we wish to bring with him.[4]

The way the various dimensions of the heart are engaged when doing mental prayer comes through most clearly when Alphonsus talks about the manner of doing so. For him, the most suitable posture is kneeling or sitting in a comfortable position. Silence is meant to permeate the entire prayer session. We begin with a period of preparation where we tell the Lord we believe in him, ask for his mercy, and make a request for light. We then move into the main body of the prayer where we reflect on how a passage of Scripture or spiritual reading pertains to our lives, get in touch with our affections regarding what we have learned, bring to God our various needs and petitions, and make appropriate practical resolutions about what to do next. The period of mental prayer then ends by thanking God for the lights received, asking him for help to carry out our resolutions, and also asking for the grace of perseverance. Alphonsus also tells us how to deal with distractions and aridities by encouraging us not to focus on or be discouraged by them but by simply letting them go

---

[4] Ibid., 87-92.

when they occur and being resolute to persevere in prayer.

Alphonsus's approach to mental prayer engages the whole person. It is concerned with posture, time, and place; it encourages us to reflect; it asks us to delve into our feelings and affections, it asks us to have solitude of heart; it can be done either alone or in the company of others; it can be done while walking in God's creation, while working or gardening. When doing mental prayer, the most important thing for Alphonsus is to empty ourselves of worldly desires and offer every part of ourselves to God. The ultimate goal in all of this is to be one heart with the heart of Our Lord.[5]

Alphonsus and The Way of the Cross

Although Alphonsus cannot be credited for creating the spiritual exercise commonly known as the *Way of the Cross*, we *can* say that he developed one of its most popular forms, so much so that it is still used in many Churches today, especially during Lent. Its roots go back to the practice among

---

[5] Ibid.

Christians in the early centuries of visiting the holy places in Jerusalem where Jesus suffered and died. When access to the Holy Land was cut off for Christians during the time of the Crusades, the practice was brought to Europe so that Christians could meditate on the fourteen stations of Jesus' passion. St. Alphonsus published his version of the stations in 1761, when he was 65 years of age. They were widely distributed and remain one of his most popular devotions to this day.

How to Pray the Way of the Cross

Alphonsus begins by telling his readers how the go about praying the devotion. He says we should kneel before the altar, make an act of contrition, and have the intention of receiving whatever indulgences associated with the practice. A set prayer follows that tells Jesus of our desire to love him with all our heart and ends with the words, "My Jesus, I will live and die always united to Thee."[6]

After this opening prayer, fourteen stations follow, each of which has a set opening dialogue

---

[6] Liguori, *Way of the Cross*, 481.

Chapter Two: Exploring the Human Heart

between the leader (preferably a priest or deacon) and the remaining participants. After each station the congregation kneels and says:

> V. We adore Thee, O Christ, and praise Thee.
> R. Because by Thy holy cross, Thou hast redeemed the world.[7]

A meditation follows where the priest names the station and invites the faithful to recite together a meditation specifically designed for it. After the meditation, they all pray an *Our Father,* a *Hail Mary,* and a *Glory Be.* After these prayers, they all stand, and the leader moves to the next station as everyone sings a stanza from the *Stabat Mater* or some other appropriate penitential hymn until they reach the next station. If possible, the priest is accompanied by three servers, one of whom carries the cross and the other two lighted candles. The fourteen stations are works of art and placed at different areas of the church, usually along each side of the nave and sometimes along the back. They can also be placed outside along a path or walkway. The idea is that those present are

---

[7] Liguori, *Way of the Cross,* 481.

participating in a pilgrimage and walking with Jesus praying to him and asking for mercy as he suffers and dies for them. The names of the fourteen stations are:

1. Jesus is condemned to death.
2. Jesus is made to bear his cross.
3. Jesus falls the first time under his cross.
4. Jesus meets his afflicted mother.
5. The Simon of Cyrene helps Jesus carry his cross.
6. Veronica wipes the face of Jesus.
7. Jesus falls the second time
8. Jesus speaks to the daughters of Jerusalem.
9. Jesus falls the third time.
10. Jesus is stripped of his garments.
11. Jesus is nailed to the cross.
12. Jesus dies on the cross.
13. Jesus is taken down from the cross.
14. Jesus is placed in the sepulcher.[8]

At the end of the stations, the leader and servers return to the altar; the participants recite more *Our Fathers*, *Hail Marys*, and *Glory Bes*. The holy exercise

---

[8] Liguori, *Way of the Cross*, 481-91.

ends with another verse if the *Stabat Mater* or another suitable penitential hymn.[9]

When viewed under the lens of an anthropology of the heart, it is clear this devotion engages the bodily senses through movement, art, and music. It also uses dialogue, traditional vocal prayers, and meditations that touch the mind, imagination, memory, and affections in a way that gives those present a deep sense of walking with Jesus and suffering with him as he carries his cross, dies on it, and is laid in the tomb. When done well, moments of quiet are spread throughout the practice that touch the spirit and inspire those present to open their hearts to Jesus' heart, which was pierced with a lance and poured out for their sake. The devotion can be practiced privately or in a group, so it also addresses the communal dimension of our human makeup. Since it can be practiced outside, it also engages the environmental dimension of our existence. Even when it is celebrated in a sacred space such as a church or chapel, we are reminded of Jesus' intention to bring about a New Creation in which all time and space will them-

---

[9] Liguori, *Way of the Cross*, 491.

selves become sacred sanctuaries for God's people to inhabit.

Alphonsus, we must recall, considers meditating on Jesus' passion and death to be one of the most important subjects of mental prayer. Outside of the Liturgy itself, which immerses us in Jesus' paschal mystery, his *Way of the Cross* is one of the most concrete and popular ways for us to meditate on the redeeming action of Christ and to respond to his exhortation, "If any want to become my followers, let them deny themselves and take up their daily and follow me" (Lk 9:23).

Conclusion

The human heart has many dimensions—physical, psychological/intellectual, spiritual, communal, and environmental—all of which are fully integrated and act as one. Jesus and his mother Mary had pure hearts. Most of us, by way of contrast, have divided hearts. For this reason, we must turn to them and ask them for a healing that will make us whole. Such healing comes through the grace of the Spirit and his manifest gifts and fruits. Mary, as we say in the *Hail*

Mary, is "full of grace." Such is God's desire for us, as well: to be full, even overflowing with grace! How does this happen? Just as our physical heart pumps life-giving blood throughout our body and removes unwanted waste, so the other dimensions of our heart pump life-giving grace throughout the dimensions of our human makeup.

Alphonsus de Liguori was aware of the multi-faceted nature of the human heart. We can see this in both his approach to mental prayer and in the way he instructs his readers to practice his *Way of the Cross*. These holy exercises touch upon each of the dimensions of the human heart mentioned above and do so in a way that both heals the heart of its wounds and opens it up to God's grace. They are but two examples of how Alphonsus's approach to prayer opens us up to God's Kingdom which is within us and in our midst, already present, yet still to come. When taken together, they show us that Alphonsus's focus on fundamental conversion of heart (*metanoia*) embraces the whole person and seeks to turn us away from worldly attachments and follow instead the way of the Lord Jesus.

Prayer, for Alphonsus, is the primary means by which this personal conversion of heart comes about. It is the great means of salvation, the way we make our way to God and find our place in Christ's Mystical Body. In the next chapter, we will explore the various types of personal prayer and examine why Alphonsus chose in his writings to concentrate on its ascetical rather than its mystical forms. He considered the former the "meat and potatoes" of the spiritual life, something which deepens our friendship with Christ and, in so doing, helps us to better understand and appreciate the importance of the Church's sacramental liturgy for our lives.

Chapter Three

Prayer, The Great Means of Salvation

If the goal of Alphonsus's ministry was the conversion of heart (*metanoia*)—a turning of our hearts to Christ and opening to his grace so that he might dwell in our hearts and we in his— then the question arises: How exactly does this come about? The answer, for him, was prayer. In 1759, he published *Prayer, the Great Means of Salvation*,[1] which numbers among his most important works and which remains to this day one of the greatest treatises on prayer ever written. In this chapter, we will explore Alphonsus's teaching on prayer presented in this book, as well as the distinction and important differences between ascetical and mystical prayer.

---

[1] Alphonsus de Liguori, *Prayer, The Great Means of Salvation*, in The Complete Ascetical Works of St. Alphonsus de Liguori, ed. Eugene Grimm, vol. 3 (Brooklyn, Redemptorist fathers, 1927), 9-250.

Personal and Liturgical Prayer

Before we continue, however, we must remember that Alphonsus was concerned for those people who had little access to the sacraments because there were few priests in his day who wished to minister in the remote hilltop villages of southern Italy. He founded the Redemptorists as a missionary congregation precisely to meet the needs of those who were poor and abandoned by the Church. Because these people could not frequent the sacraments through no fault of their own, Alphonsus focused on personal prayer as the primary means through which they could find their way to God.

As we shall see, Alphonsus presupposes the central role the Mass and other sacraments play in the life of the Church. In *Prayer, the Great Means of Salvation*, however, he focuses on prayer as the way we can draw closer to God, especially during those times when we have little or no access to them. An intense life of personal prayer, he believed, would deepen our thirst for the sacraments. When seen in this light, personal and liturgical prayer are intimately related: personal prayer increases our hunger and thirst for the sacraments; the sacraments, in turn, deepen our intimacy with Christ who, as head of the Church, blesses each of her members with his Spirit, the soul of the Church.

Alphonsus's emphasis on the centrality of the Eucharist for our spiritual lives comes through most clearly in his *Selva: On the Dignity and Duties of the Priest* (1760).[2] In it, he has this to say about what the Second Vatican Council refers to as the "source and summit of the Christian life:"[3] "All the honors that the angels by their homages, and men by their virtues, penances, and martyrdoms, and other holy works, have ever given to God could not give him as much glory as a single Mass."[4] Referring to St. Bonaventure, he says, "…in each Mass God bestows on the world a benefit not inferior to that which he conferred by his incarnation."[5] He goes on to quote St. Augustine, "O venerable dignity of the priests, in whose hands, as in the womb of the Virgin, the Son

---

[2] Alphonsus de Liguori, *Selva: On the Dignity and Duties of the Priest* in The Complete Ascetical Works of St. Alphonsus de Liguori, ed. Eugene Grimm, vol. 12 (Brooklyn, Redemptorist Fathers, 1927), 13-423.

[3] Second Vatican Council, *Lumen gentium*, no. 11.

[4] Alphonsus de Liguori, *Selva: On the Dignity and Duties of the Priest*, 209.

[5] Ibid., 210.

of God became incarnate!"[6] St. Thomas Aquinas (c. 1225-74), he says, taught that the sacrifice of the Mass is an application and renewal of the sacrifice of the cross,[7] while St. John Chrysostom (c. 347-407) says: "The celebration of a Mass has the same value as the death of Christ on the cross."[8] Clearly, for Alphonsus, nothing could replace the Mass as the central act of Christian worship, one that, as St. Bonaventure once said, was "a compendium of all God's love and of all his benefits to men."[9] The question Alphonsus raises in *Prayer, the Great Means of Salvation* is how can we deepen our spiritual lives when we do not have access to this great sacrament—and even when we do!

Having placed Alphonsus's emphasis on personal prayer in the context of its relationship to liturgical prayer, and in particular the Eucharist, we can now turn to his teaching on personal prayer as an important way for us to find our way to God. Prayer, we might say, is like breathing. We cannot go through life on a single breath, but must breathe at all times.

---

[6] Ibid.
[7] Ibid.
[8] Ibid., 211.
[9] Ibid.

As the Apostle Paul says in his First Letter to the Thessalonians, "Rejoice always, pray without ceasing, give thanks in all circumstances" (1 Thes 5:16-18).

The Great Means of Salvation

Alphonsus dedicates *Prayer, The Great Means of Salvation* to Jesus and Mary, and he underscores the importance of the work in his Introduction: "I do not think that I have written a more useful work than the present, in which I speak of prayer as a necessary and certain means of obtaining salvation, and all the graces that we require for that object. If it were in my power, I would distribute a copy of it to every Catholic in the world, in order to show him the absolute necessity of prayer for salvation."[10] Alphonsus defines prayer as simply having recourse to God. It entails *petition* (asking for particular things), *supplication* (asking for indeterminate things), *obsecration* (a solemn oath invoking the name of the Lord), and

---

[10] Alphonsus de Liguori, *Prayer, The Great Means of Salvation*, 19.

thanksgiving (gratitude to God for gifts received).[11] Without prayer, we would not be able to resist temptation and live a virtuous life. We need God's grace to live a life of holiness. God does not give such assistance unless we ask for it. For this reason, we must bring to God all our needs and do so persistently and with perseverance. Alphonsus divides his treatise into two parts. The first contains three chapters and deals with the necessity and power of prayer, as well as the conditions necessary to make it effective. The second has four chapters and shows that grace is given to everyone and focuses on the manner in which it ordinarily operates.

Part One

Chapter I: The Necessity, Power, and Conditions of Prayer. In this first chapter, Alphonsus says that prayer is a necessary means to salvation. Without it, we would not be able to resist temptations and keep the commandments. He says that to achieve this end it is helpful to have recourse to the intercession of the saints, the souls in purgatory, and especially the

---

[11] Ibid., 21-22.

Blessed Virgin Mary. Alphonsus concludes this chapter with one simple rule of thumb: "He who prays is certainly saved. He who prays not is certainly damned."[12] Another way of saying this is that those who pray will one day find themselves in the presence of God and see him face to face. Those who do not, however, will spend eternity trying to fill a big hole in their souls with all sorts of allurements, pleasures, and creaturely comforts, but which in the end only God himself can fill.[13]

Chapter II: The Power of Prayer. Here, Alphonsus points out the excellence of prayer and its power with God: "God wills us to be saved; but for our greater good, he wills us to be saved as conquerors."[14] We are in a continual state of spiritual warfare. Through the power of prayer we arise victorious against the temptations of the evil one: "It [prayer] is a weapon sufficient to overcome every assault of the devil; it is a defense to preserve us in every danger; it is a port where we may be safe in every tempest; and it is at the same time a treasure which provides us with every good."[15]

---

[12] Ibid., 49.
[13] Ibid., 23-49.
[14] Ibid, 51.
[15] Ibid., 52.

Alphonsus ends this chapter with a stark warning: "…to save one's soul without prayer is most difficult, and even (as we have seen) impossible, according to the ordinary course of God's Providence."[16] The grace to pray, he maintains, is given to everyone. Those who fail to have recourse to God have no one but themselves to blame. What is more, Alphonsus tells us that it is not necessary to retreat to the desert or to go on long fasts to pray: "What does it cost to say, My God, help me! Lord, assist me! Have mercy on me! Is there anything more easy than this? And this little will suffice to save us, if we will be diligent in doing it."[17] If we are not saved, the fault is ours alone, because we failed to pray.[18]

Chapter III: The Conditions of Prayer. In this chapter, Alphonsus discusses the conditions for prayer necessary for it to be efficacious. He says we must pray for ourselves, asking for things necessary for salvation and do so with piety and perseverance. We should also pray for others, especially if they are sinners in need of sorrow for their sins. In addition to praying with humility and confidence, Alphonsus

---

[16] Ibid., 63.
[17] Ibid.
[18] Ibid., 50-64.

says we must persevere in our prayers: "Individual prayers will obtain the individual graces which they as of God; but unless they are persevering, they will not obtain final perseverance."[19] Such perseverance does not come all at once because but only gradually. God does so because he wishes us to demonstrate our confidence in him, desire it more fervently, and remember our need for him. If we wish to be saved, we must have our eyes on the Lord at all times.[20]

Part Two

Chapter I: God Wishes All Men to Be Saved, and Therefore Christ Died to Save All Men. In this first chapter of Part Two, Alphonsus points out that "God wishes everyone to be saved."[21] He says that this is the judgment of the Church over time, and he points to various sayings of the Apostle Paul and other Scriptural texts, as well as the saying of the Fathers, to back up his claims. He also says that Jesus Christ died to save us and looks to Scripture and the teaching of the Fathers to support his position. Children who die

---

[19] Ibid., 94-95.
[20] Ibid., 65-104.
[21] Ibid., 106.

before receiving baptism do not receive the beatific vision but are united with him via their natural capacity to know and serve him.[22]

Chapter II: God Commonly Gives to All the Just the Grace Necessary for the Observance of the Commandments and to All Sinners the Grace for Conversion. In this chapter, Alphonsus offers proofs from the Latin and Greek Fathers, as well as from Sacred Scriptures, that God gives all who believe in him the grace to keep his commandments and all sinners the grace necessary for conversion.[23] He leaves those who remain obstinate in their sinful ways to their own whims and desires. He wills their salvation but cannot force them to go against their own will. God leaves these hardened sinners to themselves. He forces no one to follow him and allows us to choose our own destiny.[24]

Chapter III: An Exposition and Confutation of the Jansenist System. In this chapter, Alphonsus refutes the Jansenist position that sufficient grace to pray is not given to everyone but only to a select few and that, as a result, not everyone has the power to keep

---

[22] Ibid., 106-32.
[23] Ibid., 133.
[24] Ibid., 133-60.

the commandments. Alphonsus refutes this position and expounds the authentic teaching of St. Augustine that God does not command the impossible and thus gives everyone sufficient grace to pray as a precursor of efficacious grace, which ultimately empowers us to follow God's commands.[25] Alphonsus lays out the weaknesses in the Jansenist system and preserves human free will while avoiding the extremes of Jansenism, on the one hand, and laxism on the other.[26]

Chapter IV: God Gives All Men the Grace to Pray If They Choose. This "Sufficient Grace" Is Common to All Men and Is by Itself Enough for Prayer. In this final chapter of the treatise, Alphonsus examines the various theologians who hold that everyone receives sufficient grace to pray. He also looks at the presence of this teaching in Scripture, the Fathers of the Church, and the Council of Trent. He goes on to list the various reasons that justify this teaching and concludes with the following statement: "I say, and repeat, and will keep on repeating as long as I live, that our whole salvation depends on prayer; and,

---

[25] Ibid.,199.
[26] Ibid., 161-200.

therefore, that all writers in their books, all preachers in their sermons, all confessors in their instructions to their penitents, should not inculcate anything more strongly than continual prayer."[27]

Being a prudent and practical man, Alphonsus ends his treatise with a series of prayers, meditations, and brief heartfelt sayings that, when said with sincere piety and devotion, will help us to open our hearts to God and allow him to share his heart with ours. By sharing such prayers with his audience, he offers concrete, holy exercises for his readers to implement in their daily lives. At the end of the day, prayer must be practiced, not merely studied. Prayer, for him, is a theandric action of both God and man. It is the primary means by which God enters our lives and helps us to walk the way of holiness.[28]

The Various Grades of Prayer

For Alphonsus, it was important not only to see prayer as the great means of salvation but also to understand its various grades. An admirer of the

---

[27] Ibid., 240.
[28] Ibid., 241-50.

spiritual writings of Teresa of Avila, he was knowledgeable in all the grades of prayer, both ascetical and mystical, but concentrated on the former since we all have access to this kind of prayer. Mystical prayer, by way of contrast, depends entirely on God himself: we can do nothing about it. As we have seen, while everyone receives sufficient grace to pray, the difference between ascetical and mystical prayer has to do with who is the primary agent acting. In ascetical prayer, we receive God's assistance but remain the primary persons acting. In mystical prayer, however, the Holy Spirit takes over and becomes the primary actor. Although we all have access to the various grades of ascetical prayer, we can do nothing about mystical prayer since God dispenses these special graces to as he pleases. Alphonsus is quick to point out, moreover, that holiness does not depend on whether we have been blessed with experiences of mystical prayer. There are many canonized saints who lived holy lives without ever having had a single mystical experience. He encourages us to pray without ceasing and to strive to live virtuous lives.

We are all called to follow the threefold way of purgation, illumination, and the union. These stages of the spiritual journey do not relate in a linear fashion (as if we leave one stage behind before entering the next), but in what is more like an upward spiraling motion that repeats itself again and again but in smaller and smaller rotations until we ultimately reach the summit in a single point. We are all called to one day see God face to face in the beatific vision. God blesses some, however, with mystical visions of himself in this present life to encourage us to persevere in our own spiritual journey. The mystics, in other words, give us a foreshadowing of what we ourselves hope to experience in the life to come. Our journey into God, moreover, will never end since he is infinite and there will always be more and more of him to discover .

Ascetical Prayer. There are four kinds of ascetical prayer. *Vocal prayer* uses words that are voiced aloud either alone or with others. *Mental prayer* reflects on the mysteries of the faith using words, either privately or when gathered as a group, in the quiet of one's mind. *Affective prayer* goes deeper than merely reflecting on the faith and its relevance for our lives because it involves opening our hearts and sharing our feelings and emotions with him. *Acquired recollection* or *acquired contemplation* (as it is also called) is wordless prayer. It involves simply being quiet and resting in the presence of the Lord. It can be done alone or together, in the quiet of one's room, while taking a walk in God's creation, or while sitting in chapel before the Blessed Sacrament.

Each of us has a unique relationship to God, one that cannot be replaced or duplicated and is sustained by our prayer lives. We are called to incorporate each of these forms of ascetical prayer into a special rhythm that characterizes God's presence in our lives. This rhythm of prayer will be unique to each of us and will reflect God's singular presence in our hearts. Since these various forms of ascetical prayer presuppose faith in God, and since faith is an infused virtue that requires grace, it follows that we cannot pray without God's assistance.

Mystical Prayer. Following the teaching of St. Teresa of Avila, Alphonsus recognized various forms of mystical prayer. Mystical prayer is contemplative in nature since it involves communing with God without using words. As pointed out earlier, the Holy Spirit himself takes over when a person is in the throes in mystical prayer. When seen in this light, contemplative prayer can be either ascetical (as in acquired recollection, which each of us can do with the help of God's grace) or mystical (since it involves not merely assistance of God's grace, but also the Holy Spirit, who acts directly on the powers of the soul). Alphonsus, as we have seen, focuses on the various forms of ascetical prayer since these forms are more or less within our control. Be that as it may, he thought it important that confessors and spiritual directors be familiar with the various forms of mystical prayer so that, in the very least, they might be able to recognize them when they encounter them in someone under their care.

There are five forms of mystical prayer. *Infused Contemplation* happens when the Holy Spirit enlightens the mind, and we see everything through his eyes. The *Prayer of Quiet* happens when the Holy Spirit not only inhabits our intellect but our will as well and does so in such a way that we want nothing else than to unite our will with God's. The *Prayer of Union* happens when the Holy Spirit inhabits not only our intellect and will but also our internal senses of memory and imagination. When this happens, everything we remember and imagine happens under the direct influence of the Holy Spirit. *Spiritual Betrothal* occurs when the Holy Spirit enters not only our internal senses but our external senses as well. When this happens, we have the experience of standing outside of ourselves in a state of ecstasy. Finally, in *Spiritual Marriage*, the Holy Spirit lifts us beyond ourselves into the life of the Holy Trinity. Even though the Creator/creature relationship remains in such a state, we experience ourselves as being completely one with God. The state of spiritual marriage can be likened to the beatific vision, the main difference being that it occurs on this side of death rather than in the afterlife. Once again, mystical prayer is a gift that God bestows as he pleases and, unlike ascetical prayer, is something we can do nothing about. For this reason, Alphonsus focused his ministry on the ascetical forms of prayer. They are, we might say, the meat and potatoes of the spiritual life and, after the sacraments, are the primary means by which we receive spiritual nourishment in our daily lives. They may, to some extent, prepare us for receiving the gratuitous graces of mystical prayer, but they cannot cause it to happen. Even the great mystics returned time and again to vocal, mental, affective, and acquired recollection. They are to the spiritual life what breathing is the life itself in our earthly pilgrimage.[29]

Conclusion

Alphonsus calls prayer "the great means of salvation." For him, this insight holds true for personal *and* liturgical prayer, both of which are intimately ordered to each other, and which enable us to open our hearts to God. Conversion of heart (*metanoia*), he maintains, is the goal of the spiritual life and comes about primarily through prayer, which is essential to all Christian spirituality. With it, we will be able to walk the way of holiness and eventually find our way to God. Without it, we will lose our spiritual bearings and get lost in our pilgrimage through life.

In his book *Prayer, the Great Means of Salvation,* Alphonsus outlines some of the most basic principles of prayer and the spiritual life. Everyone, he says, receives sufficient grace to pray. If we pray, we will be saved, and if we don't pray, we will be lost. Prayer

---

[29] For Alphonsus's treatment of the various forms of ascetical and mystical prayer, see Alphonsus de Liguori, *Guide for Confessors*, ed. Richard Schiblin (Esopus, NY: Redemptorist Fathers, 1978), 111-48.

enables us to turn to God and follow his will in our lives. It empowers us to keep his commandments, live virtuously, manifest the gifts of the Spirit in our lives, and respond to his holy promptings. Divided into two parts, Alphonsus's book discusses the necessity of prayer, its power, and the conditions necessary for it. He also reminds us that God wishes everyone to be saved, is generous in dispensing his graces, refutes the errors of the Jansenists, and upholds the doctrine that God gives everyone enough grace to converse with him as a friend. He maintains that it is easy to pray and that it is the basic *sine qua non* of the spiritual life.

Alphonsus was aware of the distinction between ascetical and mystical prayer and knew of their various forms. He also knew that contemplative prayer was the hinge or linchpin between the two. A mystic in his own right, he focused on ascetical prayer because he knew it was the meat and potatoes of the spiritual life and that, with the help of God's grace, everyone could practice its various forms. He was also aware that we could do nothing about mystical prayer itself since it was up to God alone to dispense it to those as he saw fit. Ascetical prayer, he maintained, might possibly prepare us to receive such mystical gifts but could in no way cause us to receive them. Although we are all called to see God face to face in the beatific vision (*visio Dei*) in the life to come, God blesses some individuals with deep mystical experiences in this present life to build up our faith and give us a foretaste of things to come. Our journey into the mystery of God will be never ending since God is infinite, and there will always be something more of him to discover. In the final analysis, Alphonsus was a man of prayer who understood the essential role it played in God's providential plan for our salvation. Prayer, for him, was the great means of salvation. That is why he urged his readers to cultivate their friendship with God through deep, constant, heartfelt prayer.

Chapter Four

Friendship with God

As "the great means of salvation," prayer's primary goal is friendship with God. Jesus himself once said, "No one has greater love than this, to lay down one's life for one's friends" (Jn 15:13). "Friendship" is another one of those words that today is much overused. When saying it, we can be referring to almost anyone or anything: someone we may recognize on the street, a casual acquaintance, a friend on Facebook, a pet (as in a dog is "man's best friend"), a true friend. There are different grades of friendship and, indeed, different types. In this chapter, we will explore what it means to be "friends of God." As pointed out earlier in this book, this was the name given to the saints in the early Church. Jesus wants to befriend us in order to make us holy. He wants us to be saints. We become so by doing what friends do: spending time with each other, talking with one another, sharing our innermost thoughts and feelings with each other.

The Four Loves

Before discussing friendship itself, it would be helpful to look at it against the backdrop of the other kinds of love. In his book *The Four Loves*, C.S. Lewis (1898-1963) identifies these four as affection (*storge*), friendship (*philia*), romantic love (*eros*), and charity (*agape*)—each of which has a particular focus.[1] Affection, for example, represents the natural feelings we have toward family members, such as a father's affection for his son and a mother's affection for her daughter. These affections rise naturally from the bonds of family and larger clan or kinship. Friendship, which we will study in more detail later in this chapter, arises from a commonly shared goal as in a hobby or sport. Here two friends share a common interest and bond with each other as a result of this shared love. Romantic love arises when two people "fall in love" and look into each other's eyes with a kind of ecstasy or madness. The phrase being "madly in love" reflects the way people in love are drunk with love for one another. Charity is the selfless love one

---

[1] See C. S. Lewis, *The Four Loves* (San Diego: Harcourt, Brace, Jovanovich, 1960), 53-192.

Chapter Four: Friendship with God 63

has for others. It is a willingness to lay down one's life for another without weighing the cost and without expecting anything in return. Jesus' death on the cross represents the epitome of sacrificial love and serves as the model for his followers to strive after.

It bears noting that, with some exceptions (e.g., a parent's affection coupled with a romantic love for one's offspring), these loves are not mutually exclusive. A father, for example, can love his son with parental affection and, in time, become his son's friend. Two lovers can eventually become friends, while two friends may one day fall in love. It is also worth noting that each of these loves is found in God. He is, at one and the same time, a father to us, as we find in the Lord's Prayer (*storge*), madly in love with us, as we see in *The Song of Songs* (*eros*), a friend to us, as Jesus refers to his disciples in the Gospel of John (Jn 15:15) (*philia*), and a selfless giver, as we read in the Passion narratives (*agape*). Some theologians such as Søren Kierkegaard (1813-55) and Anders Nygren (1890-1978) believed that friendship, being preferential, could have nothing to do with charity which, they would say, was non-preferential by its very nature. Others, however, such as Augustine of Hippo,

Aelred of Rievaulx (1110-67), and Thomas Aquinas assert that friendship is not opposed to charity but a deeper incorporation into it. Aquinas, in fact, refers to charity as "a kind of friendship of man for God."[2]

As far as friendship is concerned, Aristotle (384-322 BC) tells us in his *Nicomachean Ethics* that there are three types: those of pleasure, those of utility, and those based on goodness and virtue.[3] In friendships of pleasure, people are drawn to each other out of a common interest that gives them pleasure and makes them feel good. It could be something as simple as going to the movies, listening to opera, belonging to a book club, or cheering on a favorite sports team. They have bonded with one another because of their pursuit of a certain kind of pleasure that they share with one another. Friendships of utility are formed because they are useful to each other. For example, two people study together to prepare for a test and get a good grade. They help on another out of a

---

[2] See Wadell, *Friendship and the Moral Life*, 70-119. For the quotation from Aquinas, see Thomas Aquinas, *Summa theologiae,* II-II, q. 23, a. 5, resp.

[3] Aristotle, *Nicomachean Ethics*, 1156a10-24; 1056b6-22. See also Wadell, *Friendship and the Moral Life*, 51-69.

common interest and receive something useful in return. Although they can be sincere and even lasting, friendships of pleasure and utility pale in comparison to those based on goodness and virtue. These friendships are the deepest, most authentic kinds of friendship, for they are based solely on living the good life, which, according to Aristotle, are the key to what he calls *eudaimonia*, a state of complete well-being that leads to happiness. For Aristotle, *eudaimonia* is the goal (*telos*) of life. Since we are social beings by nature, we seek to lead the good, virtuous life and do so with the help of others. Such friendships are also called friendships of character. We bond with others out of our common interest to build character by becoming good. For him, virtue is the key to human happiness.

Christian Friendship

Christians live in the world but are not of it. They adopt anything in the culture around them that is inherently good and condemn anything that is evil. This holds true also for the world of thought. They baptize those ideas that can help explain the Gospel message to their peers and do so by transforming them with the knowledge of and wisdom of Christ. With regard to friendship, Christians have used Aristotle's approach to help unravel the mystery of our relationship with Christ.

Of the three types of friendship developed by Aristotle—those of pleasure, utility, and character—thinkers like Aelred of Rievaulx and Thomas Aquinas have taken friendship based on a good and virtuous life (i.e., character) and transformed it into "friendship with Christ." They embrace the beloved words of Augustine, who says in his *Confessions*, "O God, you have made us for yourself, and our hearts are restless until they rest in you."[4] Christ alone is the source of true happiness. Nothing else compares with being in a close, intimate friendship with him. Jesus told his disciples that he no longer called them servants but now looks on them as his friends (Jn 15:15). This holds true as much for his present-day disciples as it did for the first. But what precisely does it mean to be a "friend of Christ."

---

[4] Augustine of Hippo, *Confessions,* 1.1.

Chapter Four: Friendship with God

According to Aquinas, there are three primary marks of friendship: benevolence, reciprocity, and mutual indwelling.[5] Benevolence means not only wishing good for others, but also actively seeking their well-being. To have friends means that we look out for them and do our best to promote their cause. Reciprocity means that our friendships must be mutual. There is no such thing as a one-way friendship. If our desire for friendship is not matched by a similar desire, then there is no use in pursuing it. By its very nature, friendship is a two-way street. If the friendship is not reciprocal, then it is not a friendship at all. Mutual indwelling refers to the experience of carrying one's friend in one's heart—and vice versa. Aristotle once described a friend as "a second self."[6] The sentiment behind this metaphor is very much on target. Close friends care for one another in such a way that each lives for the other and sees the other's good as their own. History is full of examples of close friendships: David and Jonathan, Basil of Caesarea

---

[5] See Thomas Aquinas, *Summa theologiae*, II-II, q. 23, a. 1, resp.; II-II, q. 24, a.11, resp. See also Wadell, *Friendship and the Moral* Life, 130-41.

[6] Aristotle, *Nicomachean Ethics*, 1170b10.

and Gregory Nazianzen, Francis and Clare—to name but a few. True friends wish each other well and actively seek the other's well-being; they share a mutual care and regard for one another; and they carry the other within them wherever they go.

Christian friendship is not at odds with Christian charity. The two complement one another and reveal what it means to spread the Gospel. Jesus gave his life for the salvation of the world yet still had a few close friends. Mary, his mother, was probably his closest friend and follower. Lazarus and Mary Magdalen would also number among those with whom he shared deep friendships. Peter, James, and John were also disciples whom he singled out from the others and considered close. Jesus went about spreading his message by calling a handful of disciples, twelve in all, whom he called his apostles and to whom he entrusted the building up of his kingdom after his departure from the earth. When Jesus walked the earth, he satisfied his very human need for friendship by singling out a few men and women from the many others he had called to confide in them and share with them some of his deepest, innermost thoughts. He once told them that he and his Father were one

Chapter Four: Friendship with God 69

(Jn 10:30), and he wished to share that intimate unity of souls with them. Jesus left this world so he could send us the Holy Spirit. With the Spirit in our midst, Jesus is able to befriend each and every one of us in a way that he was unable to do when he walked the earth. When in the flesh, Jesus could have close, intimate friendships with only a select few. Once he ascended into heaven and sent the Holy Spirit to the nascent Church, he could dwell within the hearts of all who believed in him. That is to say, we all have the opportunity to be close, intimate friends with him in the way that he shared close, intimate friendships with Mary, his mother, Lazarus and Mary Magdalen, Peter, James, and John, and possibly a few others. With the coming of the Holy Spirit, Jesus extends the hand of friendship to all who call upon his name and recognize him as Lord.

Conversing with God

Close friends spend time together and talk with one another about things that matter to them. They are able to get past the superficial and go down deep. In an earlier chapter, we have seen how much

Alphonsus valued making visits to the Blessed Sacrament. We have also seen his emphasis on prayer as "the great means of salvation." To understand how easy he thought it was to talk to God, we will now examine his popular treatise *The Way to Converse Always and Familiarly with God* (1754).[7]

Alphonsus divides his treatise into five parts: (1) God Wishes Us to Speak with Him, (2) It Is Easy and Agreeable, (3) Of What, When, and How, (4) God Answers the Soul that Speaks to Him, and (5) A Practical Summary. His goal in this work is to give us an easy way to talk with God and to emphasize that anyone can talk with him at any time and in any place.

God Wishes Us to Speak with Him. In this first section, Alphonsus emphasizes how much God loves us and how mistaken we are when we think that approaching him with confidence and familiarity is a lack of reverence. On the contrary, God wants to befriend us and encourages us to share our most intimate thoughts with him. He is, at one and the same

---

[7] See Alphonsus de Liguori, *The Way to Converse Always and Familiarly with God*, in *Talking with God*, 3-34.

time, both Infinite Majesty, and Infinite Goodness and Love. No one, Alphonsus goes on to say, loves us more than God. He loves each one of us as if we were the only person in the world. To show us the extent of his love for us, he emptied himself, entered our world by taking on our humanity, suffered and died for us, and gave us his very flesh and blood to eat and drink. He took on our humanity so that we might share in his divine life. Alphonsus then gives us one of his most famous passages: "'My delights are to be with the children of men' (Prov 8:31). The paradise of God, so to speak, is the heart of man. Does God love you? Love him. His delights are to be with you; let yours be to be with himself, to pass all your lifetime with him, in the delight of whose company you hope to spend a blissful eternity. Accustom yourself to speak with him alone familiarly with confidence and love, as to the dearest friend you have, and who loves you best."[8]

It Is Easy and Agreeable. In the next section, Alphonsus goes on to say how easy and enjoyable it is to converse with God. It is a mistake, he says, to think

---

[8] Alphonsus de Liguori, *The Way to Converse Always and Familiarly with God*, 7.

we must always look to God with fear and trembling. Look at the saints: "Ask those souls who love him with a true love, and they will tell you that in the sorrows of their life they find no greater, no truer relief, than in a loving converse with God."[9] God is closer to us than we think. He travels before us to show us the way, behind us to catch us when we fall, beside us to accompany us on our journey, and within us to rejoice with us in our successes and to comfort us in times of trial. What is more, he always takes the first step. When we desire his love, he gives us the grace to open our hearts to him and reveal to him our deepest desires and concerns. He says: "There is no barrier at the door against any who desire to speak with him; no, God delights that you should treat with him confidently. Treat with him of your business, your plans, your griefs, your fears—of all that concerns you. Above all, do so (as I have said) with confidence, with open heart."[10] Although God is everywhere, Alphonsus says that there are two places above all

---

[9] Alphonsus de Liguori, *The Way to Converse Always and Familiarly with God*, 8.

[10] Alphonsus de Liguori, *The Way to Converse Always and Familiarly with God*, 8-9.

Chapter Four: Friendship with God

where he has his own special dwelling: in "the highest heaven" and in "the humble soul that loves him."[11] He is always present to us and desires nothing more than to open our hearts and make ourselves present to him.

Of What, When, and How. In the third section, Alphonsus deals with the circumstances during which our conversations with God take place. We can and should speak to him as often as we can since he never grows weary of us and invites us to converse with him as often as we like. In times of trial, we should present our afflictions to him, and he will comfort us in our time of need. At such times, we should remind ourselves that he is our Redeemer, can bring good out of evil, and uses our trials as a way of drawing us closer to him. When we are joyful, we should share our happiness with him and invite him to rejoice with us. Still, we should rejoice more in his blessedness than in our own good fortune. After we have committed some fault, we should not be ashamed to go to him and ask his forgiveness. He tells his readers: "Attend greatly, devout soul, to the

---

[11] Alphonsus de Liguori, *The Way to Converse Always and Familiarly with God*, 10.

instruction commonly given by masters of the spiritual life, after you unfaithful conduct, at once to have recourse to God, though you have repeated it a hundred times in a day; and after your falls, and the recourse you have to the Lord…at once be in peace."[12] When in doubt, we should still treat God as our closest friend and share with him our uncertainty. Close friends consult one another at such times. At such times, we should ask God to enlighten us and help us decide what to do. We should also bring him not only our own needs and petitions, but also those of others. We should pray especially for those who are suffering in the present, those in purgatory, and those who do not yet know him. We should also express to God our yearning to be with him in heaven and to tell him how much we yearn to share eternal life with him. Alphonsus reminds us that God always answers those who speak to him: "In a word, if you desire to delight the loving heart of your God, be careful to speak to him as often as you are able, and with the

---

[12] Alphonsus de Liguori, *The Way to Converse Always and Familiarly with God*, 20.

Chapter Four: Friendship with God

fullest confidence that he will not disdain to answer and speak with you in return."[13]

Practical Summary. In the final section of the treatise, Alphonsus sums up everything he has said and offers advice that will help us live in a way pleasing to God. To begin with, he tells us to raise our minds to God when we wake in the morning and to raise and offer to him everything we do. In addition to going to confession, receiving Communion, and praying the Divine Office, he encourages us to offer God everything else we do such as work and study, and ask him for help to carry out our duties in a manner pleasing to him. He encourages us to keep ourselves ever in a state of recollection by raising our hearts and minds to God in everything we see and hear. He also encourages us to allow the infant Jesus to be present in our meditations. Just as he was born into the world some 2,000 years ago, he now wishes to be born within our hearts. What is more, Alphonsus encourages us to make an offering of ourselves to God each and every day. Whenever we are about to decide on something, we should first ask for the

---

[13] Alphonsus de Liguori, *The Way to Converse Always and Familiarly with God*, 24.

Lord's guidance and then go about our business. In short, he counsels us to occupy ourselves, as the saints do in heaven, only with God and to do everything for his glory. While living in this world, we are to occupy our minds with God alone. Only then will our desires be perfectly fulfilled and satisfied.

Conclusion

Friendship (*philia*) is one of the four loves, the others being: natural affection (*storge*), which rises out of natural family bonds; romantic love (*eros*), which happens when two people fall madly in love with one another; and charity (*agape*), which is selfless love, as in laying down one's life for a friend. Friendship differs from the three in that it focuses on a common interest shared by two people. With few exceptions, these four loves are not mutually exclusive. What is more, they all exist in God since he is variously described in Scripture as Father, Lover, Friend, and Savior. Because we are made in the image and likeness of God, we are able, with God's grace, to imitate Christ and both think and act as he did. As the Apostle Paul says, "…it is no longer I who live,

Chapter Four: Friendship with God

but it is Christ who lives in me" (Gal 2:20). Charity, itself, has been described as "a kind of friendship of man for God." The basis of Christian friendship is fellowship with Christ, who also unites us to his Father in a bond of the Spirit.

There are three primary marks of friendship: benevolence, reciprocity, and mutual indwelling. A friend wishes his friend well and actively seeks his or her well-being. Such a friendship must also be mutual and culminates in a sense of living in each other's heart. God's deepest wish is to befriend us. He did not give up on us when we fell from grace and turned away from him. Rather, he had his Son enter our world to live among us, suffer, and die for us, so that we might once again enjoy fellowship with him. In other words, in the person of Jesus, God actively seeks our well-being and wants us to love him in return so that he can live in our hearts. God entered our world some 2,000 years ago so that he could enter each of our own private worlds, dwell within our hearts, and allow us to dwell in his.

In his treatise *The Way to Converse Always and Familiarly with God*, St. Alphonsus reminds us that prayer is simply opening our minds and hearts to

God. God wants us to speak with him in this way. He says it is easy to do and agreeable and can be done at any time and in any place. We should share with him our trials and joys, as well as our faults and doubts. He says we should pray for others and tell him how much we wish to be with him in heaven. He also reminds us that God always answers the prayers of those who speak with him, although not necessarily in the way we might expect. "The paradise of God," he reminds us, "is the heart of man." Friendship with God, in his mind, lies at the very heart of the Gospel message.

Chapter Five

Paradise for God

In this final chapter, we will take a deep dive into what the phrase "The paradise of God, so to speak, is the heart of man" might mean. To do so, we will need to ask ourselves how God's immutability and impassibility can be reckoned with the mystery of his Incarnation. We will also examine how "paradise for God" differs from human paradise, as well as how they overlap. This leads to the question of how God's love for us in Christ differs from our love for God through Christ. Finally, it will look at the similarities and differences between our journey into Christ's sacred heart and his journey into ours.

Our Immutable, Impassible, and Incarnate God

According to the Catholic tradition, God is immutable and impassible. That is to say, he can neither change nor suffer. If this is so, then the question arises: How do these statements correlate with the mystery of the incarnate Christ who suffered and died for us? The two positions seem to be mutually exclusive.

At the very start, it is important for us to recognize that, according to the doctrine of the Trinity, God the Father is transcendent; God the Son, incarnate; and God the Holy Spirit, immanent. Co-eternal with the Father, the Son is eternally begotten by God and became human to redeem us from our sins. The Holy Spirit, Co-eternal with the Father and the Son, proceeds from them from all eternity and was sent to Jesus' followers after his ascension into heaven. These three Persons exist in One God and represent an intimate community of Love that has existed from all eternity. This community exists out of time and is immutable by its very nature. At the same time, certain actions flow from them that take place within time and space and are involved with the transient nature of the created world, these being Creation, Redemption, and Sanctification. Although God *always* acts as one, the Father is typically associated with the act of Creation; the Son with the act of Redemption; and the Holy Spirit with the act of Sanctification. When seen in this light, God's immutability and impassibility are tied to the way that he interacts with his Creation.

Chapter Five: Paradise for God

Another way of dealing with this is to say that God's love is self-diffusive. God's love, in other words, freely flows out of his immutable, unchanging nature in the threefold activity of Creation, Redemption, and Sanctification. When seen in this light, God is immutable by nature, yet capable of interacting with his transient, mutable, and finite creation. In fact, he holds his Creation in his hands and sustains it moment by moment. This is a rather ingenious way of preserving God's unchanging nature while allowing him to interact with the world he created. It represents a juxtaposition of the Greek philosophical understanding of an unchanging, immutable Prime Mover with the Hebrew concept of a God as the Lord of History who intervenes throughout time in a covenantal relationship with his people. This unique juxtaposition preserves the mystery of God by employing, at one and the same time, both positive (cataphatic) theology and negative (apophatic) theology in an uncanny "coincidence of opposites" that underscores both the limits of human language and our inability to fully exhaust the mystery of the One Source from whom all things flow.

According to the doctrine of Christ's hypostatic union, Jesus' divine and human natures are united in the One Divine Person, the Eternally Begotten Son of the Father, while remaining distinct from one another and without change or confusion. This union was defined at the Council of Chalcedon in 451 A.D. and enabled the Council fathers to steer clear of the heretical doctrines that tended to mix the two natures or deny Christ's divinity. The doctrine preserves Christ's full humanity and full divinity making him, at one and the same time, both the Son of Man and Son of the Father. This union of the human and divine natures is used to explain how Jesus, being fully human, experienced the various stages of growth involved in human existence and even suffered and died, and yet in his divinity remained immutable and impassible in his union with the Father and the Holy Spirit.

Jesus' Threefold Love

The hypostatic union is a key lens for understanding the human and divine loves in Jesus. In his encyclical *Delixit nos*, Pope Francis speaks of the being three loves in Jesus' Sacred Heart: "The image of the Lord's heart speaks to us in fact of a threefold love. First, we contemplate his infinite divine love.

Then our thoughts turn to the spiritual dimension of his humanity, in which the heart is "the symbol of that most ardent love which, infused into his soul, enriches his human will." Finally, "it is a symbol also of his sensible love."[1] These three loves are distinct by virtue of Jesus having two separate natures, yet intimately united in him in his Divine Personhood and Sonship.

Pope Francis continues: "These three loves are not separate, parallel or disconnected, but together act and find expression in a constant and vital unity. For 'by faith, through which we believe that the human and divine nature were united in the Person of Christ, we can see the closest bonds between the tender love of the physical heart of Jesus and the twofold spiritual love, namely human and divine'"[2] Jesus' love for us is both human and divine. He does not love us sometimes in his humanity and at other times in his divinity. These three loves, while distinct, always act in close harmony with each other.

---

[1] Pope Francis, *Delixit nos*, no. 65; Pius XII, Encyclical Letter *Haurietis Aquas* (15 May 1956), II: AAS 48 (1956), 327-328.

[2] Ibid., no. 66; 343-344.

Let us now look at these three loves in more detail. As the Eternal Son of the Father, Jesus' divine love exists from all eternity and is closely linked with the love of the Father, as well as that of the Spirit. By virtue of the hypostatic union, this divine love of the Son is distinct from yet intimately related to the two loves of Jesus' human nature, the one seated in his rational appetite, the will, and the other in his sensible appetite. Jesus' love for us, in other words, is both human and divine. Since he always acts as one, it is fruitless to try to isolate one from any of the others. His love for us is transformative. That is to say, it plumbs the depths of our humanity and, through his humanity, allows us to participate in his divinity. In this way, our love for him becomes divinized by virtue of our being members of Christ's Mystical Body, the Church. Because he is infinite, his love for us can never be exhausted. What is more, the four loves cited earlier in an earlier chapter—*storge*, *eros*, *philia*, and *agape* —are united to Jesus' human and divine loves and give us an even deeper insight into the mystery of God's love for us.

Paradise for God

After having examined both the relationship between the divine and human natures of Christ and the various kinds of love in his Sacred Heart, we are now in a position to look at the meaning of the phrase, "the paradise of God is, so to speak, the human heart." At the outset, we must understand that the word "paradise" is used analogously when it is applied to both God and man. For human beings, "paradise" is something we yearn for and hope one day to attain. It represents the epitome of human happiness and reaches fulfillment not in the present life (although we may, at times, be blessed with a taste of it) but only in the life to come. It is an eschatological, already-but-not-yet, reality, something we hope one day to possess in its entirety. For God, on the other hand, "paradise" is not something to one day be attained but is already present in him in all its fullness. If "paradise" stands for the vision of God (*visio Dei*), then God possesses this vision and has no need whatsoever of anyone or anything else. His love is infinite and fully self-contained in and of itself.

At the same time, it is also important for us to remember that Jesus always acts as one and that the various loves noted above exist in close harmony with one another. Jesus' human loves, both spiritual and sensible, participate in his divine love and are divinized by it. When seen in this light, Jesus' human love is different from ours since we are affected by the consequences of sin—original, social, and personal—and he is not. His human love represents what we long for and are tending for. Jesus entered our world and became one of us so that he could enter the world of our hearts, offer us his friendship, dwell within them, and divinize them by uniting our humanity with his by means of the close rapport with his divine nature. To "divinize" our hearts does not mean to make us divine, but to purify them and make them holy and godlike, so we can share in the intimate love of the Blessed Trinity.

So, what does the phrase "paradise for God" actually mean? As pointed out earlier, it is not something that God lacks in any way. He does not *need* to dwell in our hearts to achieve happiness. He is love itself and already has happiness to the full. He is his own *telos*, his own end. At the same time, because he is love itself, he wishes to share that love and does so, not only in the immanent relations within the Trinity, but also through the threefold actions of

Creation, Redemption, and Sanctification. These actions are not necessary in the sense that they had to take place. They are freely chosen acts of God's self-diffusive love. The creative action of the Father happens drop by drop (*guttatim*) from one moment to the next. The redemptive action of the Son heals and renews creation when it went awry through Adam's fall from grace. The sanctifying action of the Holy Spirit transforms us into holy beings, adopted sons and daughters of the Father. To say that God's paradise is to dwell in the human heart means that God loves humanity, the pinnacle of creation, not only from without but also from within. He created us in his own image and likeness so we could love him in return. He has no need of our love, but we have need of his. Without it, we would never become the people we are called to be.

The Two Journeys

The mutual indwelling of hearts made possible by the friendship between Jesus and us is a dynamic rather than static relationship. Each friend journeys into the depths of the other's heart. Each of these journeys is unique, although they also share some similarities. They are alike in that they are both rooted in love. C.S. Lewis draws a distinction between "gift love" and "need love."[3] The former has to do with the giving of self while the latter concerns being able to receive love. Each of these is necessary in an authentic friendship. Both must be able to give of oneself and receive the other's love in return. The difference between Christ's love and ours is that our capacity to both give and receive is limited because of the corruption of sin and our limited human nature while his is unlimited by virtue of his divine nature and his untainted human nature.

The relationship is also dynamic in the sense that our journey into God never ends. In *The Life of Moses*, Gregory of Nyssa introduces the concept *epektasis*, the idea that our journey into God is unending because God is infinite and knowledge him cannot be exhausted by his creatures.[4] Our journey into God, in other words, will never end since there will always be something more to discover about him. For this same reason, our journey into the heart of Christ will go on for all eternity. What is more, this

---

[3] C.S. Lewis, *The Four Loves*, 11-21.

[4] Gregory of Nyssa, *The Life of Moses*, 2.239.

journey will send us deeper and deeper into the divine mystery and will be the source of unending enjoyment for us. Our journey into the mystery of the divine will be a source of incommensurable joy for us.

Jesus, by way of contrast, already knows everything about us and, in fact, knows us better than we know ourselves. His journey into our hearts is finite in the sense that he already knows us through and through. There is nothing more for him to discover about us. In another sense, however, it is infinite in that he accompanies us on our journey into *his* heart. He does so by shedding light upon the path before us and expelling whatever darkness we encounter during our earthly sojourn. In the life to come, moreover, he journeys with us as we together explore for all eternity the Divine Mysteries from which all things come.

Alphonsus and the Divine Indwelling

Although God had no need of it, he has freely chosen to make our heaven his heaven. He has poured his love into the heart of man and has made our human joy his joy. "Paradise for God," in other words, is another way of saying that, out of love for us, God has decided to make our happiness his—and vice versa. He entered our world in Jesus Christ to wed his divinity to our humanity and, in doing so, was able to enter the world of the human heart, befriend it, and dwell within it. He does this through the indwelling of the Holy Spirit, the Third Person of the Blessed Trinity, who proceeds from the Father and the Son and who represents the deep love shared between them.

In his *Novena to the Holy Spirit*, Alphonsus shows us what this indwelling does to our hearts.[5] In his Introduction, Alphonsus says, "This novena consists of meditations and prayers to be used for the feast of the Ascension of Jesus into heaven until the feast of Pentecost. It is the most important of all novenas if only because it was the first ever to be observed and celebrated in the Church."[6] All in all, it has ten meditations, each of which is to be prayed on the days preceding the descent of the Holy Spirit

---

[5] Alphonsus de Liguori, *Novena to the Holy Spirit* in From the Heart of Saint Alphonsus: Favorite Devotions from the Doctor of Prayer, 1-22.

[6] Alphonsus de Liguori, Novena to the *Holy Spirit*, 1.

Chapter Five: Paradise for God

upon the nascent Church, as well as throughout the liturgical year. They are:

1. Love is a fire that inflames the heart.
2. Love is a light that illumines the human spirit.
3. Love is a fountain that satisfies our thirst.
4. Love is a dew that enriches our soul.
5. Love is a repose that refreshes.
6. Love is a virtue that gives us strength.
7. Love causes God to dwell within us.
8. Love is a bond that unites.
9. Love is a treasure that contains every good.
10. How we can love God and become a saint.[7]

From the titles of these meditations, it is clear that the indwelling of the Holy Spirit is the same as the indwelling of God's love within our hears. The purpose of the Spirit's dwelling within our hearts is to make us holy, to make us saints, to make us "friends of God."

By dwelling within our hearts, the Spirit endows us with his manifold gifts and fruits. These bring us

---

[7] Alphonsus de Liguori, *Novena to the Holy Spirit*, 4-22.

a joy and a peace that the world cannot give. They give us a foretaste of paradise and enable us to walk in the footsteps of Our Lord throughout our earthly sojourn until we reach our yearning for God reaches fulfillment. Such is God's paradise: to dwell within our hearts. He does so not because he needs to but only because he loves us. His paradise is very different from ours but, because of Jesus, the Word-made-flesh, also very similar. God dwells in our hearts so that we might dwell in his and share in his infinite love forever with our finite, creaturely hearts.

Conclusion

The word "paradise" is used analogously when applied to God and man. That is to say, there are both likenesses and differences when comparing them. Because God is immutable and impassible, he is infinite, cannot change, and has no need of anyone or anything other than himself. Heaven, for him, is nothing other than himself. The Blessed Trinity thus needs nothing, for it forms from all eternity an intimate and infinite community of love. Because he is love itself, however, God's creates, redeems, and sanctifies freely rather than out of necessity. It is in this sense that his love is self-diffusive: He creates, redeems, and sanctifies purely out of love—and for no other reason.

The Son of God became human to conquer death and free us from our sins. This, too, was done purely out of love rather than necessity. He took on our human nature and was like us in all things but sin (Heb 4:15). This nature was united to his divine nature by means of a unique hypostatic union, which united the two in the One Person of the Son, keeping them distinct and allowing them to maintain their own qualities. As Pope Francis reminds us, Jesus' Sacred Heart was thus infinite by virtue of his divine nature, and both volitional and sensible by virtue of this human nature. Because of this divine Incarnation, "paradise" for God now shares certain similarities to what it means for us. Through Jesus, the Word-made-flesh, God now joins us on our earthly sojourn as we travel to our heavenly homeland. He goes before us to show us the way, behind us to catch us when we fall, beside us to accompany us on our journey, and within us to dwell there in an intimate friendship rooted in Jesus' passion, death, resurrection, ascension, and descent of the Holy Spirit upon the Church.

God entered our world to dwell in our hearts so that we could share in his divinity through his humanity and become adopted sons and daughters of the Father. St. Alphonsus, in his *Novena to the Holy Spirit*, captures the unbounded beauty of God's love for us. He created us in his image and likeness precisely so we could freely return his love and become his close, intimate friends. As a result, he now lives in the hearts of all who welcome him. We, in turn, now dwell in his heart and through our participation in his glorified humanity can now share in the mutual love he shares with his heavenly Father as his adopted sons and daughters.

Conclusion

We have likened Alphonsian Spirituality to a two-edged sword. One edge of the sword is a "Spirituality of Practice" which has already been treated in the first book of the trilogy, *Holy Exercises*. The other edge of the sword concerns his "Spirituality of Heart" and has been the subject of this second book of the trilogy, *Paradise for God*. These two edges of the sword come together in a point and reveal Alphonsus's "Spirituality of Mission," which will be treated in the trilogy's final book, entitled *Going Forth*. The idea behind his spirituality is that our devout practices should be designed to touch our hearts and lead us on to mission of preaching the Gospel in both word and deed.

In these pages, we have seen that Alphonsus's understanding of heart is in line with the traditional Biblical understanding of the heart as the center of a person's spiritual energy and thought as it opens up to God. We have used the thought of Hans Urs von Balthasar and Pope Francis to deepen our understanding of heart as it is reflected in Alphonsus's thought. We have also used the insights of Aristotle, Aelred of Rievaulx, Thomas Aquinas, C.S. Lewis, and others to show that the purpose of the heart is to open itself up to friendship with Christ and the indwelling of the Holy Spirit. We have seen that such friendship is not opposed to selfless love (*agape*) but complementary to it. We have also seen that "paradise for God" is unique yet, because of the mystery of the Incarnation, is also like what heaven is for us. The Son of God entered our world and became human so he could enter the world of our hearts, befriend us, divinize us, and make us adopted sons and daughters of the Father.

Alphonsian spirituality is all about conversion of heart. We cannot preach a Gospel of conversion if we ourselves have not opened our hearts to God in friendship. We cannot give what we ourselves do not possess. We cannot invite others to receive Jesus' personal friendship if we have not opened or own hearts to him and allowed his Spirit to dwell there. Mission is preceded by holy exercises and heartfelt conversion. The three go together and must not be separated. The Gospel is spread and the world changed one heart at a time. Let it be so both now—and forever!

www.ingramcontent.com/pod-product-compliance
Lightning Source LLC
Chambersburg PA
CBHW060846050426
42453CB00008B/858